Cousin Chaos:

Laughing with my Cousins

M. S. Gregory

Copyright © 2025
by Tried and Trusted Indie Publishing

ISBN: 978-1-923623-08-8
All rights reserved.
Cover designed by msgdragon

No part of this publication may be reproduced, distributed, or transmitted in any form or by any means, including photocopying, recording, or other electronic or mechanical methods, without the prior written permission of the author, except non-commercial uses permitted by copyright law.

Also by M. S. Gregory

- Cousin Chaos: Laughing with your Cousins
- Sibling Shenanigans: Laughing with my Sister
- Sibling Shenanigans: Brother-Sister Jokes
- Mum Seriously!! Teen-mum banter at its finest!
- What Cats really Think: Hilarious Cat Thoughts, Jokes, and Conversations That Will Make You Laugh
- From Bark to Snark: Sassy thoughts from your Pup

For permission requests, address the request to the author c/o
Permissions,
TAT Indie Publishing
triedandtrustedindie@gmail.com

My cousin challenged me to a staring contest.
Three seconds in, he laughed. Turns out, he's really good at blinking strategically.

I asked my cousin to babysit. He said, "No problem!"
The kid ended up babysitting him instead.

Cousins are like magnets.
They attract trouble, and sometimes snacks.

My cousin said, "I can cook better than you."
Five minutes later, smoke alarms were cheering him on.

Cousins are the only people who can insult you and still get a hug immediately after.

I asked my cousin to keep a secret.
He whispered it so loudly, even the neighbor knew.

My cousin tried to be serious for five minutes.
I missed it. He never tried again.

Cousins are like pajamas.
Comfortable, familiar, and occasionally cover weird stains.

I asked my cousin for directions.
He said, "Just follow the chaos." And somehow, it worked.

Cousins are like superheroes.
They appear out of nowhere, usually with a snack or a prank.

My cousin said he's good at puzzles.
We bought one together. I'm still finding pieces under the couch.

Cousins always know your embarrassing stories.
And they're not afraid to tell them... in song.

I told my cousin I was scared of spiders.
He gave me a magnifying glass... and a bug collection book.

Cousins are proof that family therapy exists in every laugh.

My cousin said, "I'm teaching you responsibility."
Then he stole my candy. I'm learning fast.

Cousins are like Wi-Fi signals.
Strong in some rooms, weak in others, but you always need them.

My cousin asked if I wanted to start a club.
I said yes. Turns out, it's the "Laugh at Everything" club.

Cousins are experts at sneaking snacks.
And even better at blaming it on you.

I asked my cousin to teach me a trick.
He taught me how to hide cookies in plain sight.

Cousins make the best co-conspirators.
And the worst alibis.

Cousins are the best cheerleaders.
They'll clap for your success, and laugh at your mistakes simultaneously.

Cousins are like sunglasses.
You don't need them all the time, but life is brighter with them.

I told my cousin I was cold.
He gave me a sweater... from last century.

My cousin loves math.
He counts my snacks before I eat them.

My cousin said he could fix my phone.
Now it's in airplane mode... permanently.

I asked my cousin why he's always late.
He said, "Time waits for no one... except me."

My cousin said he's a master of hide-and-seek.
I found him in the laundry basket... asleep.

Cousins always know your weird habits.
And they call them by fun nicknames.

I told my cousin to watch my dog.
He tried... but the dog trained him instead

Cousins are proof that chaos comes in family-sized portions.

My cousin said, "I'll help you with your homework."
He drew doodles instead. Homework still isn't done.

Cousins are like secret agents.
They know all your missions… and leak the fun ones to everyone.

I asked my cousin to teach me patience.
He said, "Wait while I prank you first."

My cousin challenged me to a joke contest.
He won… with a knock-knock joke from 1998.

Cousins make family photos interesting.
One wink, one goofy face, and everyone else just follows.

I asked my cousin for fashion advice.
He said, "Wear whatever's clean." So helpful.

Cousins are the only people who can embarrass you
and still expect a hug afterwards.

My cousin said, "Let's play chess."
We ended up flipping the board… laughing.

Cousins are like batteries.
They recharge the family… and sometimes drain it too.

I told my cousin I was tired.
He suggested a nap… in his bed.

My cousin loves to joke about ghosts.
But he screams first, then tells the story.

Cousins always know when you've sneaked extra dessert.
And they never forget it.

I asked my cousin for a ride.
He said, "Hop in!" Then we got lost in the neighbor's yard.

Cousins are the ultimate teammates.
Especially when it comes to pranks.

My cousin tried to be serious during a movie.
I laughed. He laughed. The movie never started.

Cousins are the only people
who can call you weird and make you
laugh instead of crying.

Cousins are proof that mischief runs in the family.

I asked my cousin for a pep talk.
He said, "You're awesome... but bring snacks next time."

I told my cousin I was bad at sports.
He joined me... and we still lost together.

My cousin said he could run faster than me.
I let him go first... I still beat him to the couch.

My cousin said, "Let's bake cookies."
I said, "Great!"
We ended up with flour everywhere and no cookies.

Cousins are like magic.
They can turn a boring day into a silly adventure.

I asked my cousin to watch my plants.
He watered them with soda... now they're sparkling!

My cousin tried to teach me how to whistle.
Now we can only whistle in unison... off-key.

Cousins are like popcorn.
A little quiet at first, then suddenly, they're everywhere.

I asked my cousin for advice on being cool.
He said, "Step one: don't ask me.

My cousin challenged me to a video game.
He rage-quit after five minutes... I still lost.

Cousins always have the best stories.
Even the embarrassing ones about you.

I told my cousin I was nervous about a test.
He said, "Don't worry, I'll distract the teacher for you."

My cousin said, "I can fix your bike."
I ended up walking... but at least it's colorful now.

Cousins are like puzzles.
You never know which piece will make you laugh next.

I asked my cousin to play a quiet game.
He brought a drum set.

My cousin said, "I'll race you to the corner store."
I won… but now he's planning a rematch for revenge.

Cousins can turn a rainy day into an adventure.
And a tiny puddle into a swimming pool.

I told my cousin I was hungry. He said, "Snack attack!"
Then threw chips at me.

My cousin loves to "help" with chores.
Mostly by hiding the vacuum cleaner.

Cousins are the only people who can prank
you and still demand ice cream afterward.

I asked my cousin why he's always joking.
He said, "Serious is boring, and I'm the cure."

My cousin said he's a DIY expert.
We now have a chair with three legs… but it's "artistic."

Cousins are like adventure buddies.
They make even the shortest walk feel like a treasure hunt.

I asked my cousin to help clean the car.
He sprayed me instead. Now I'm spotless, but the car isn't.

Cousins never say "I told you so."
They just laugh until you remember it yourself.

I told my cousin I was learning guitar.
He said, "Cool! I play the radio."

Cousins are like fireworks.
Loud, colorful, and best enjoyed outdoors.

My cousin said, "Trust me, I've got a plan."
That's how we ended up stuck in a treehouse with no ladder.

My cousin said he was starting a "no sugar" diet.
He lasted three hours.
Right until Grandma brought out the cake.

Cousins are like shoes.
Different styles, different sizes—
but somehow, they always fit together.

My cousin said, "Let's make a movie!"
We filmed for ten minutes...and spent two hours
arguing over who gets the starring role.

Cousins are the only people
who can steal your fries
and make you thank them for sharing.

I told my cousin I was broke.
He said, "Same!"
Then asked if I could lend him money.

Cousins have two moods:
laughing uncontrollably or planning mischief.
There's no in-between

Cousins are like potato chips.
You can't have just one,
and they're all a little salty.

My cousin texted, "Be ready in five minutes."
That was an hour ago.
Some traditions never change.

My cousin decided to "fix" the Wi-Fi.
Now the TV speaks French.

Cousins are the perfect mix of sibling and best friend—
with just enough chaos to keep life interesting.

My cousin said, "Don't tell anyone."
So of course, everyone found out within ten minutes.

Cousins don't just make memories—
they make evidence you'll never live down.

Cousins don't just visit.
They move in emotionally and eat all your snacks.

Cousins make the best memories.
Usually because someone forgot to bring the map.

I told my cousin I was trying to be mature.
He said, "Let's race shopping carts!"
So much for that idea.

I asked my cousin to proofread my essay.
He added three jokes and a doodle.
Now my teacher thinks I'm hilarious.

My cousin said, "Let's take a shortcut."
Forty minutes later, we were lost, hungry, and arguing over the GPS.
Some shortcuts just take the long way.

I asked my cousin to be normal for one day.
He said, "Define normal."
And that's when I knew we were related.

Cousins are the only people who'll laugh at your worst ideas—
then help you do them anyway.

Cousins are like phone chargers—
you don't always see them,
but when you need them, they save your day.

My cousin said, "Let's build a fort!"
By the end, the living room looked like a disaster zone.
But it was the best fort ever built.

Cousins are proof that family and fun
can be the same thing—
especially when trouble's involved.

I told my cousin to act his age.
He said, "Which one? Mentally or physically?"

Cousins never just hang out.
They turn it into an event the neighbors still talk about.

My cousin swore he could fix the lawnmower.
Now it makes smoothies.

Cousins are the only ones who understand your family stories—
because they were usually part of the chaos.

I told my cousin I was bored.
Five minutes later, we were running from a sprinkler gone rogue.